God's Rules OK

'I fancy Princess Di. That's not adultery, is it? Why didn't she wait till she met me?'

'I wouldn't buy a fall-out shelter even if I could. I wouldn't want to come out and see what we've done.'

When is it right to turn the other cheek? Do we own *things* or do they own *us*? Do I have a conscience? And what is it, anyway?

Lying, stealing, killing, adultery . . . here is a collection of frank and hard-hitting comments from teenagers taking an honest look at the Ten Commandments and what they mean today.

God's Rules OK is written by the team who put together the best-selling *Home-made Prayers,* and illustrated with photographs taken by the boys themselves.

Janet Green has written a number of books for schools, worked on a BBC television series and been script consultant and Assistant Producer of a television documentary. She is currently Head of RE and Drama at Greenway Boys' School in Bristol and Chief Examiner for the South Western Examinations Board.

Janet Green & Co.

GOD'S RULES

A LION PAPERBACK
Tring · Belleville · Sydney

Published by
Lion Publishing plc
Icknield Way, Tring, Herts, England
ISBN 0 85648 653 1
Lion Publishing Corporation
10885 Textile Road, Belleville, Michigan 48111, USA
ISBN 0 85648 653 1
Albatross Books
PO Box 320, Sutherland, NSW 2232, Australia
ISBN 0 86760 479 4

First edition 1984

British Library Cataloguing in Publication Data

Green, Janet
God's rules OK.
1. Christian life
I. title
248.4 BV4501.2

ISBN 0-85648-653-1

Printed and bound in Great Britain by
Blantyre Printing and Binding Company Ltd,
Glasgow

Contents

Foreword

Greenway Boys' Secondary School is a comprehensive in a Bristol housing estate. It is due for closure in 1984 because of falling rolls.

In 1982 we were caught up in an experience which resulted in the book *Home-made Prayers*. The boys took the photographs which interpreted the teenage hopes and fears expressed in the prayers. They were disappointed when the book was complete.

'We'll do a follow-up some day,' I promised. 'Probably for a slightly older age group. Leavers' Prayers perhaps.'

'We're not leavers yet. What can we take photos of *now*?'

It is a standing joke in school that from the second year upwards I always include the Ten Commandments in the end-of-year examinations.

'Don't tell me. The Ten Commandments!' said one boy.

'Why not?' I said. 'Cecil B. De Mille had better watch out.'

Religious Education has changed a great deal since the days when it was known as Bible Study or Divinity. The boys know that it is more about exploring beliefs than merely explaining them. They want to understand the world in which they live. They realize that beliefs affect behaviour. They appreciate the need for tolerance and yet for developing their own personal life stance. It came as no surprise, therefore, that alongside the Christians who wanted to apply the Bible teaching to their lives, there were volunteers who were Hindus, Muslims, atheists or agnostics.

To be honest, I hadn't anticipated fully the avenues we would find ourselves exploring. We were deep into the very nature of rules themselves when the following conversation took place.

I had asked, 'When did you first learn the words 'should'

or 'ought to'? I found some budding philosophers in our midst talking about social behaviour, values and Platonic absolutes. They didn't know the appropriate vocabulary but they were fully conversant with the concepts.

'You catch on about right and wrong. First it's your parents. You get hit or shouted at if you does what they thinks is wrong. It's usually for your own good. They reckons you have to learn. Sometimes they gives you sweets. That's if you does things good.'

'Yeah. That's how you starts to learn about it. Mind you, some families have different rules. Some families thinks some things are right – to survive like – that other families says are wrong.'

'No. In the end some things are right and some are wrong. That's all there is to it. Like Hitler was wrong.'

'No he wasn't. We thought he was wrong. He did what he thought was right.'

After going round in circles they agreed to leave Hitler out of it. The two main protagonists continued.

'As you grows up you learns about right and wrong for yourself.'

'Yeah. You decides for yourself what rules to keep.'

'No. I don't mean that. There's more to it than just that. You learns about real right and wrong.'

'You mean the Ten Commandments. I'm not a Jew or a Christian or anything like that.'

Another boy joined in. 'Yeah, but everybody thinks the Ten Commandments are a good idea more or less.'

'Yeah,' someone else added, 'our laws are based on them.'

'I don't know about that. What I mean is that if the Ten Commandments hadn't been written, they'd still be true.'

'How could they be if they hadn't been written?'

'No, I mean the ideas behind them would still be true. They were true before they got written down for the Jews.'

They decided to leave the Ten Commandments out of the argument. The main speaker chose another example.

'Say like when the Jews learnt that God didn't want religion to have human sacrifice. There were still people who thought it was OK by their rules in their religions.

Even if there was no God to say it, we all know now that doing human sacrifice is wrong.'

The discussion wandered off around such topics as the death penalty and then returned to the point.

'I think there are sort of invisible rules and we gradually learn what they are. I don't think it's just the laws of the country and crime and all that – 'cos some countries have different laws. It's bigger than all that. The Ten Commandments made it easier till we get to understand better.'

He was reminded by the rest that they were leaving the Ten Commandments out of it. A lull happened in the conversation. To keep it going I asked, 'Suppose there were no people on earth. Would there still be rules?'

They rose to the bait. The thinking began again in earnest. At first they all said 'No'.

'Yes,' burst out one of them suddenly. 'If there's a God the rules would exist anyway. Like the laws of nature.'

'No, they wouldn't,' said another. 'He made the rules when he thought of making the people.'

'No. His rules are part of God. It's just the way he is.'

There was a pause. This time I didn't interrupt. I was thinking as hard as they were. One boy turned to me directly and asked, 'Do you reckon that if we believe in even just one rule being sort of forever really true that we're believing there is a God without knowing it?'

After conversations like this one, I realized there was more to our project on the Ten Commandments than taking photographs of teenagers agonizing over how to keep them.

When we are studying the Ten Commandments in class I set a task that others might like to try.

Each pupil has to make ten rules for running a perfect school. Before we begin we decide what schools are for.

When each boy has ten rules he joins with a mate. They have to produce a set of ten rules between them. The pairs join with another pair. Eventually we have a few groups of eight who have discussed until they have settled on their own ten rules.

We find some common ground emerges. Usually the

majority of rules could be classed as health and safety. We find ourselves discussing school policy about eating and smoking and explore possible alternative approaches.

'Trouble with rules,' said one boy, 'is that you can't cover all the idiot things that people are likely to do.'

His group had changed from rules beginning 'Thou shalt not' to ones starting 'You should . . .' This leads the way for the following homework: find *one* rule for running a school that would cover everything. The wording may differ but the sense of their answers is the same. They all come back with general positive principles about loving others.

Inevitably the next lesson is on the teaching of Jesus. We read Jeremiah 31:31–34 about the New Covenant (New Testament), then the words of Jesus at his Last Supper with his friends (Luke 22:20), 'This is the New Covenant in my blood.'

We turn then to Mark 12:28–34. Jesus was asked which is the greatest of the Ten Commandments. Our boys aren't surprised to find that Jesus didn't choose any particular commandment. They know themselves how the commandments overlap. Instead Jesus stated two general principles which summed up all the Ten Commandments: Love God and love your neighbour.

The Sermon on the Mount (Matthew 5–7) then shows us those principles in practice and usually we continue by reading Paul's beautiful chapter about love in I Corinthians 13.

Examination pupils go on to study 'The Conflict Stories' to see how Jesus looked beyond the letter of the Law to the spirit of its intention and beyond mere actions to the thoughts of the heart (see Appendix).

On one occasion a particular lad seemed very disgruntled.

'That's spoilt it all,' he said, 'having these general principles. You can't get round them. I likes lots and lots of rules about what you've not to do. You know where you stand – and anyway with lots and lots of rules, you've got something to break.'

By the end of our project we were discussing this urge to

break rules. I set them the task of finding out what conscience is.

'I don't know what it is,' said one boy, 'but I knows I got one. My dad's got one too, he says.'

'I don't know what it is either,' said another, 'but I think it's what makes people different; what makes them human.'

'I don't know about that,' came the reply, 'I reckon our dog's got a conscience. He knows when he's done something wrong.'

But my favourite saying about conscience came from 1C.

'Do you think it's a bit of God in us?'

This book documents our search into the meaning of the Ten Commandments for us today. We hope the photographs, comments and excerpts from written work will help others in school, church or wherever to search for answers. Like us you may find that the starting-point is learning to ask the right questions.

We decided to keep to the wording 'Thou shalt not . . .' for the commandments even though it might seem old-fashioned. This was because of our growing awareness of the links with the past.

We studied the meaning of each commandment in its Old Testament context, looked at the way it was interpreted at other times of history, then tried to apply it to today.

At the end of the study of each commandment a group of us worked on a prayer that we felt we could use.

It was a very serious project but there were lighter moments.

'What's the difference between unlawful and illegal?' asked one boy. Thinking we were off into one of our long debates we all frowned with the effort of thinking. Then we realized he was grinning.

'I'll tells you,' he laughed. 'The difference is that one is a sick bird!'

Janet Green

STREET SURVEY

A group of second year boys used their spare time to do a survey on the housing estate where they live. They asked random passers-by to tell them any one of the Ten Commandments.

For them it was a valuable exercise but it cannot be considered to be a comprehensive survey, particularly since some answers were obviously tongue-in-cheek.

The boys, however, took it very seriously and here are their findings:

Out of 124 people

15 went on to show that they knew all of the Ten Commandments

20 said they didn't know any. This included one who said, 'Sorry, son, we didn't do it at school . . .'

27 refused to answer, though the boys interpreted this as meaning that they didn't like to admit to ignorance

16 quoted 'Thou shalt not steal'

13 'Thou shalt not kill'

6 'Thou shalt not commit adultery' (or words to the same effect)

3 'Thou shalt not take the Lord's name in vain' (in the wording 'Thou shalt not swear')

3 'Thou shalt not make graven images' (in the wording 'Thou shalt not have idols')

The boys commented that God should have made the Ten Commandments easier to remember because, they felt, that was why people remembered 'Thou shalt not steal' and 'Thou shalt not kill'. They collected 21 'extra' commandments:

Thou shalt not ride a bike with no lights.
Thou shalt not have sex under age.
Thou shalt not play football.
Thou shalt not break school rules.
Thou shalt not play strip Jack naked.
Thou shalt not be stupid.
Thou shalt not cheat thy mother and father.
Thou shalt do chores.
Thou shalt not have girls or booze.
Thou shalt not kill animals for their furs.
I won't steal from God.
Thou shalt not steal from a shop.
Thou shalt not be a homosexual.
Thou shalt not cheat thy friends.
Thou shalt be good to thy friends.
Thou shalt be good to other grown-ups.
Thou shalt be good at sports.
I shalt not drink alcohol.
I want double glazing.
Whatever he says it is (from a wife whose husband had just quoted one of the commandments).

And finally . . .

'The Ten Commandments . . . yes I know them . . . Luke, John, Matthew, Mark, Paul, David . . . sorry, son, I can't remember the other four.'

What answers would you get in your area? Which Commandment comes to your mind first?

SCHOOL SURVEY

The boys of Greenway school cover the Ten Commandments in their second year course. So a second survey was conducted in school. The question was: Write down any one of the Ten Commandments. The boys are aged from 11 to 16.

As expected, the majority of the first years did not know any of the Commandments. Of the rest of the school a half instinctively quoted 'Thou shalt not kill'. Almost a third quoted 'Thou shalt not steal'. The rest were scattered about equally in their responses throughout the Ten Commandments except that nobody mentioned the graven images nor the sabbath day. 'Thou shalt not covet' got one vote. (Later we discovered he thought it meant 'Thou shalt not convert'.)

In conversation afterwards with the third year, almost all of them said that the first thing they thought of was 'Thou shalt not commit adultery' but they had felt too embarrassed to say.

The Ten Commandments are most familiar in the Authorized Version of the Bible. A more modern version is given on page 78.

And God spake all these words, saying, I am the Lord thy God, which have brought thee out of the land of Egypt, out of the house of bondage.

1 **Thou shalt have no other gods before me.**

2 **Thou shalt not make unto thee any graven image, or any likeness of any thing that is in heaven above, or that is in the earth beneath, or that is in the water under the earth: Thou shalt not bow down thyself to them, nor serve them: for I the Lord thy God am a jealous God, visiting the iniquity of the fathers upon the children unto the third and fourth generation of them that hate me; and shewing mercy unto thousands of them that love me, and keep my commandments.**

3 **Thou shalt not take the name of the Lord thy God in vain; for the Lord will not hold him guiltless that taketh his name in vain.**

4 Remember the sabbath day, to keep it holy. Six days shalt thou labour, and do all thy work: but the seventh day is the sabbath of the Lord thy God: in it thou shalt not do any work, thou, nor thy son, nor thy daughter, thy manservant, nor thy maidservant, nor thy cattle, nor thy stranger that is within thy gates: for in six days the Lord made heaven and earth, the sea, and all that in them is, and rested the seventh day: wherefore the Lord blessed the sabbath day, and hallowed it.

5 Honour thy father and thy mother: that thy days may be long upon the land which the Lord thy God giveth thee.

6 Thou shalt not kill.

7 Thou shalt not commit adultery.

8 Thou shalt not steal.

9 Thou shalt not bear false witness against thy neighbour.

10 Thou shalt not covet thy neighbour's house, thou shalt not covet thy neighbour's wife, nor his manservant, nor his maidservant, nor his ox, nor his ass, nor anything that is thy neighbour's.

Exodus 20:1–17

WHY
RULES?
'If I
had to make 10 rules
for running our house,
I wonder
what they'd be?'

You need rules
on the road
in the gym
on the pitch
at sea
in the countryside
in the workshops
in the game

★★★★★★★★★★★ School rules ★★★★★★★★★★★★★★★★★

'You shouldn't muck about with the javelin'

'What a mess this lot could make'

WHY RULES?

Dear Lord,
If we're going to live together in the world
I suppose we've got to have rules.
Otherwise, I might as well be on a desert island
all by myself.
I can see the sense of having rules on the road
and in a game;
so help me understand the reason for
the ones at home and at school.
I want to play fair
so help me keep the rules.
And if the rules are silly
show me how to go about changing them.
As for your ten rules –
they're in a league of their own.
I suppose they don't change
because you don't.
And people are much the same
then and now.
Help me as I study your Commandments;
to see what they mean
for me
today.

'Jesus came to show us what God is like;
it's better than just telling us.
Only – he left it a bit late;
there'd been a lot of history by then.
I suppose he knew what he was doing though.'

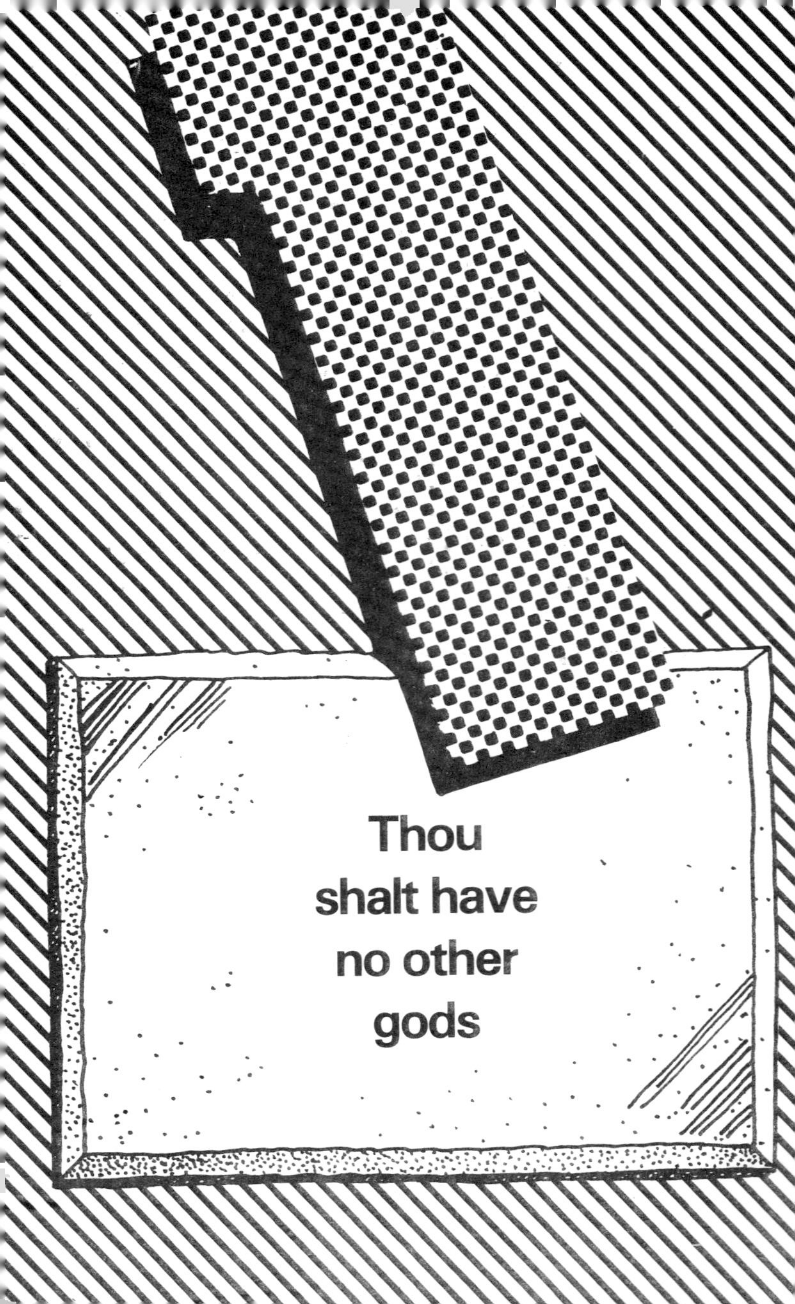
Thou
shalt have
no other
gods

'It's hard to imagine people taking those old gods seriously – especially the Greeks and the Romans. You'd have thought they'd have more sense.'

'When God said he was their God; didn't they know he was other people's God too?'

'I wish I was Jewish.
Passover sounds fun.
We've nothing like that in our house.
I'm the youngest boy in our family.
I'd get to say,
"Why is this night not like any other?" '

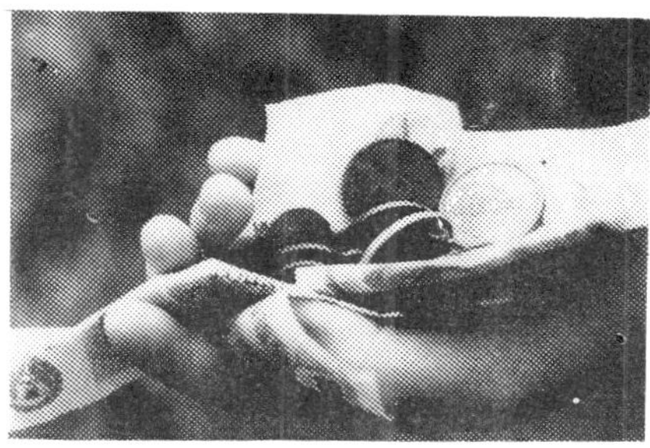

Dear Lord,
Thank you for bringing me out of my old way of life
like you brought the Jews out of Egypt.
When something like that happens,
you just know there's a God.
Help me to keep true to you
and not to wander off.
It's so easy to let other things rule my life –
even good things.
I'm not likely to want the gods they had long ago
but I've many things that are important to me.
Help me to get my loyalties in the right order.
Amen

'I am the greatest!'

Thou
shalt not
make any
graven image

'I get worried about the second commandment.'

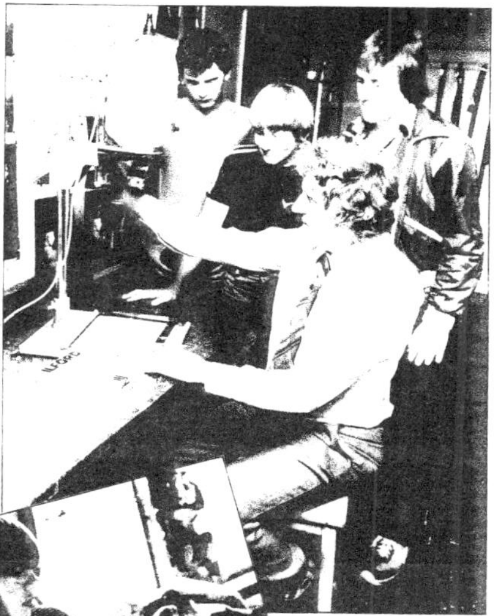

'Does photography count as graven images?'

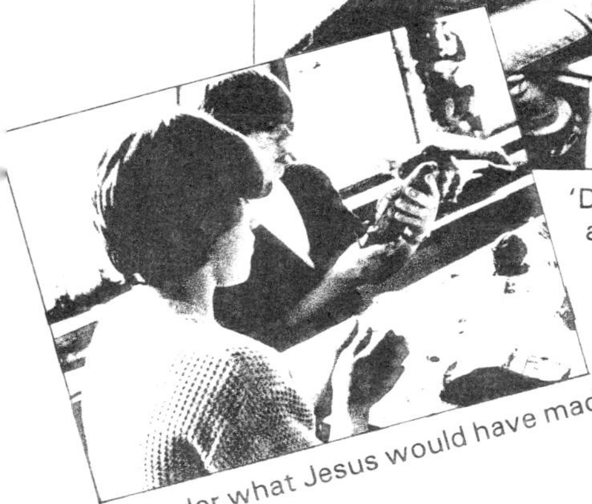

'I wonder what Jesus would have made of all this?'

2

Dear Lord,
About these statues:
it worries me.
I can understand the Jews being warned off
in those days;
but does it matter now?
I like Art lessons; they're ace –
but I'd hate to think I'm making graven images.
And what about churches?
Should they be plain?
Don't holy pictures help?
I'm not going to worship idols
if that's what's worrying you.
And I'm not superstitious –
I know that symbols aren't magic.
So what were you getting at?

The Tele-god: The one-eyed idol in our living-room.

5
Thou
shalt not take
the Lord's name
in vain

'I wonder how you swear in Eskimo.'

'I swear mostly when I'm with my mates. It's funny how you break commandments mostly when you're with your mates.'

'Sometimes my mum says,
"On the baby's life" –
'cos they thinks a lot of the baby.
That's tight that is –
suppose the baby dies?'

'Cross my heart and hope to die
Stick a needle in my eye.'

'I'm not going to say
'Cor blimey' anymore. Not now
I knows what it means.'

'I wonder if King Alfred swore when he burnt the cakes?'

'I think it's sad how all our sex words have been turned into swear words. You'd think they didn't like it.'

'The worst swearer in our family is our little 'un. She gets it off the tele.'

3

Dear Lord,
I'd try not to break a promise
I made in your name;
But there's more to it than that, isn't there?
I shouldn't need to swear on oath
if I'm honest in the first place.
Help me keep that in mind.
And as for cursing –
I know it's wrong.
Forgive me for using words carelessly
out of anger or habit –
I know I made them cheap.
Forgive me for the times
I've tried to look big – and feel big –
I know I made myself small.
Help me to remember
that you're listening too.
It sounds creepy
but it's one way of making sure
I don't let you down
when I open my mouth.

'Oops. Sorry God!'

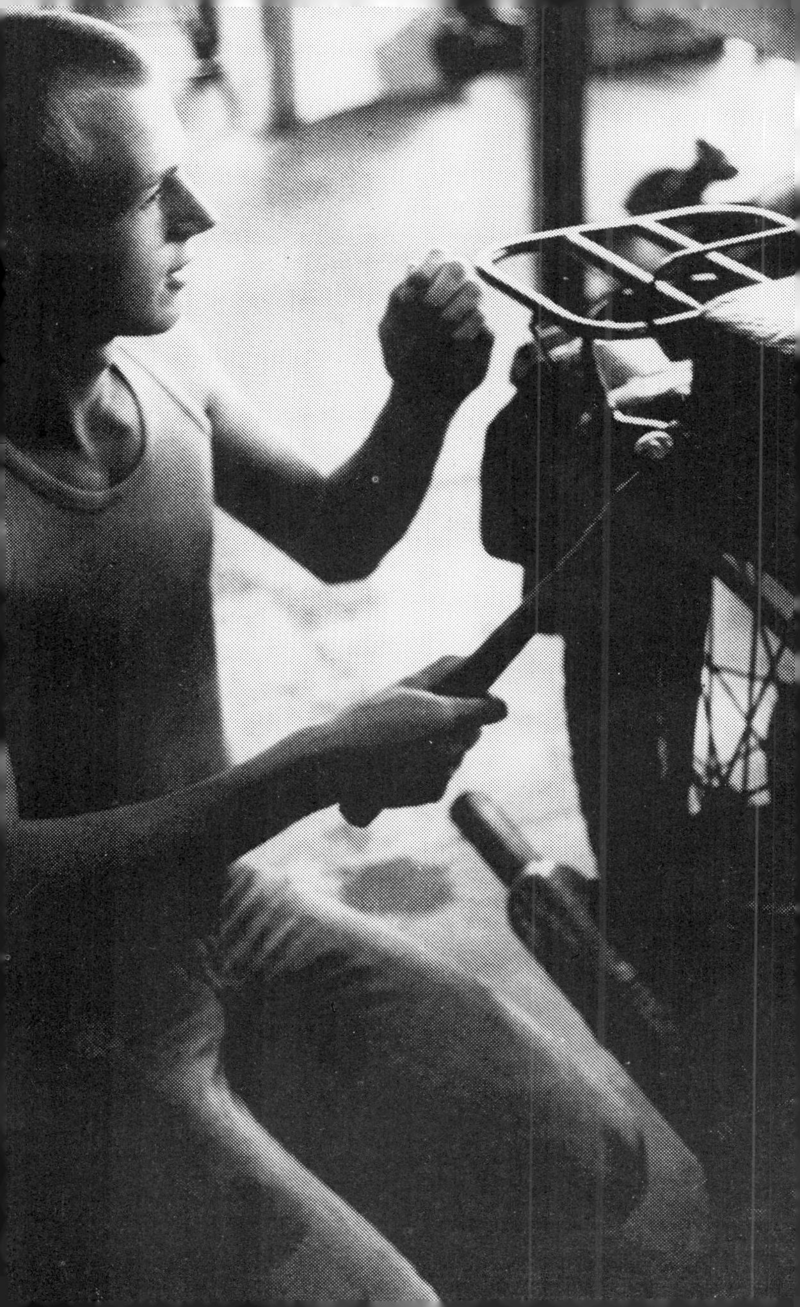

Remember
the sabbath day,
to keep it
holy

'You wouldn't think holidays started off as holy days.'

'Then we had crisps for Sunday dinner because it was work to cook the roast spuds. Now that's carrying it a bit far, that is.'

'To be really strict, maybe you shouldn't read the paper on Monday. That was made the night before.'

'What I don't get about Jesus, is why he made such a fuss when he healed that man with the funny arm. Why didn't he just do it on the quiet? Anyway – why didn't he just wait till, say, next Wednesday? I wonder what he would have had to say about Sunday trading nowadays? You never know with Jesus – he always put a new slant on things.'

4

Dear Lord,
Every day is special
now I'm following you.
But it's a good idea to have one day different,
a day of rest and change
one in every seven.
It's caught on all over the place.
For me, it's Sunday
because Jesus rose from the dead
on the first day of the week.
Help me to spend it wisely.
Guide me in deciding what not to do.
But more than that:
show me the things I should do
to make this a special day
for growing closer to you.

'If God hadn't rested on the seventh day, I wonder what else he would have made?'

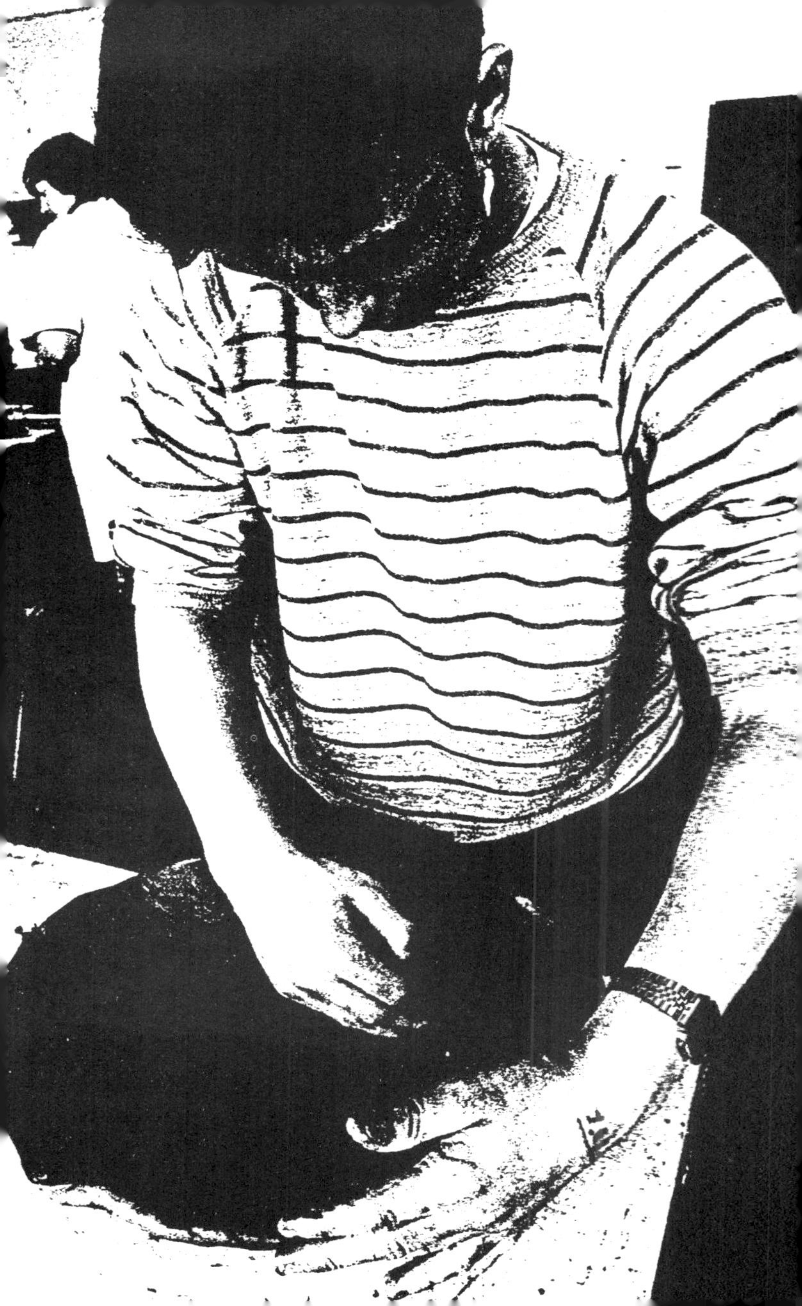

Honour
thy father
and
thy mother

In loco parentis.
'Don't tell me I've got to honour them too.'

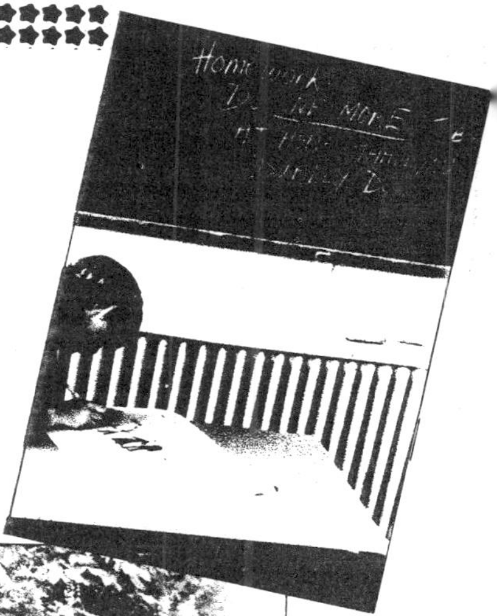

'They tell me to act my age
then treat me like a child.'

5

Dear Lord,
Help me every day at home.
Help me to show respect to my parents
out of love not just out of duty
and forgive me when I fail.
Forgive me for the times I am selfish and self-centred,
causing hurt to others in our family.
They make mistakes as well Lord –
teach me to forgive.
Help me to understand their points of view
and show me how to cope with each problem
as it comes along.
I want to get on with other people
and I know that lesson begins at home.

'You're always answering back.
I bet your friends don't cheek their parents.'

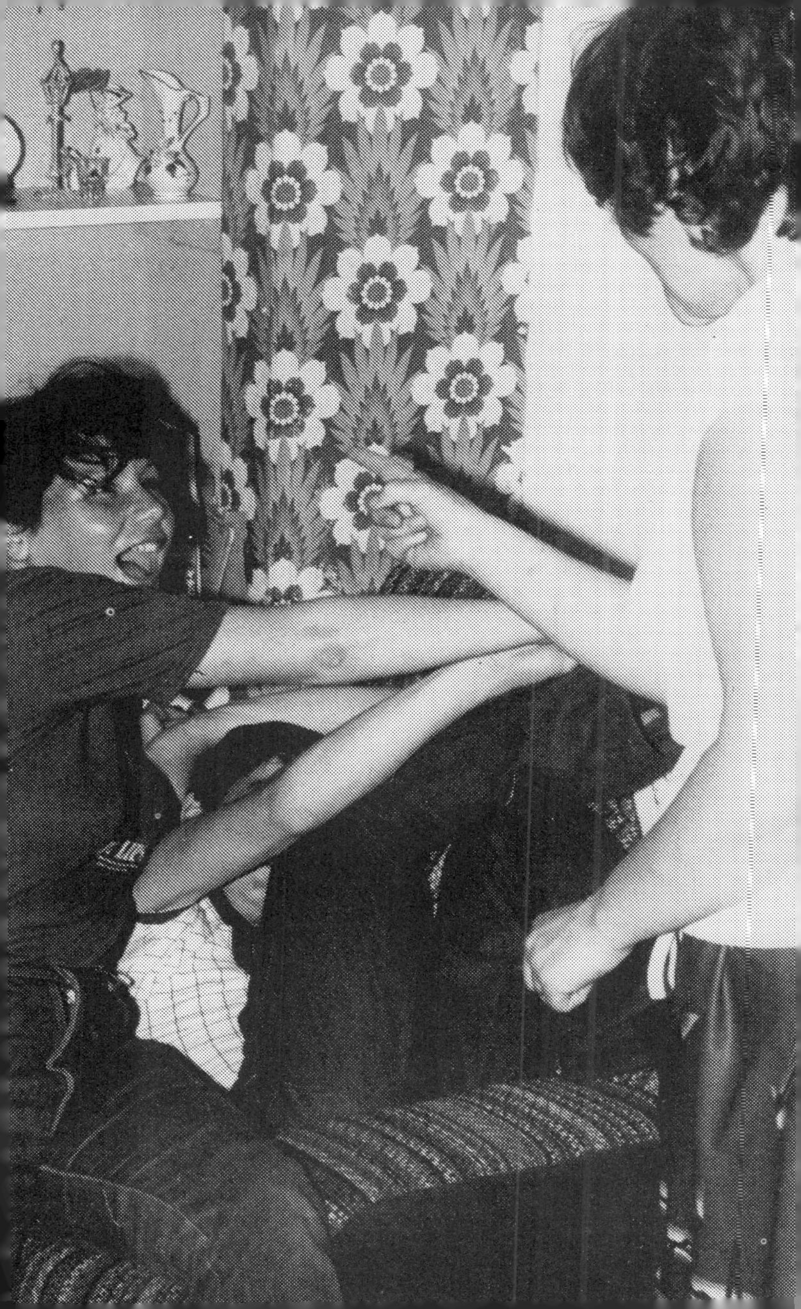

Thou
shalt not
kill

'I wouldn't buy a fall-out shelter even if I could. I wouldn't want to come out and see what we've done.'

'What a time to decide I ought to be a pacifist.'

'It doesn't count when we have war because we don't mean to kill them.'

'I know the early Christians didn't fight. But they only had those mangy old lions. We've got bombs. It took them 400 years to get the point over. We won't get that long.'

'Seventy times seven.
That's 490 times you've got to forgive.
I guess he reckoned you'd lose count
by the time you got that far.'

Dear Lord,
I haven't killed anybody
and I don't think I ever will.
It would be on my conscience,
I'd never be able to forget it all my life.
Jesus said if you hate somebody
you're guilty of murder.
It doesn't seem fair to me.
Especially when I thought I'd found
one sin I hadn't done.
That means we could all be murderers at heart.
But I suppose it makes sense really.
If there was no hating, there'd be no killing.
There'd be no wars either.
And I wouldn't be sitting here
wondering if they'll be waiting for me
outside the school gates
at quarter to four.

'Turn the other cheek.
That's suicide with this lot.'

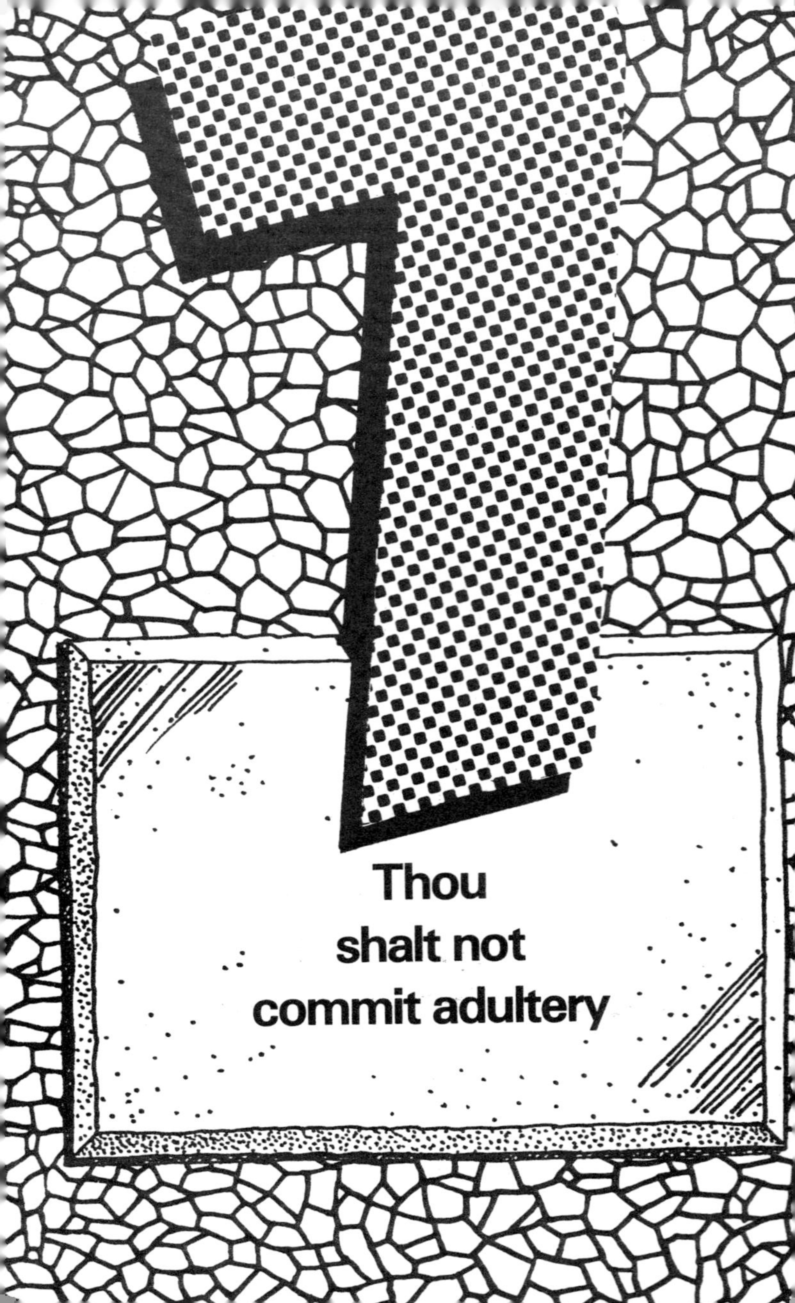
7
Thou
shalt not
commit adultery

'I fancy Princess Di. That's not adultery, is it? Why didn't she wait till she'd met me?'

'There's a difference between being in love and loving somebody. I think it's more pleasant being in love. Real love is hard work.'

'They had lots of wives in those days. I don't reckon to it. Would you be happier with seven wives? You'd have to work seven times as much.'

'What's wrong with flirting?'

7

Dear Lord,
Here's another commandment
I thought I hadn't broken;
but I might have known
Jesus would have something more
to say about it.
If thoughts count too
I bet everybody's broken this one –
I know I have.
Help me in all my relationships
not to use people selfishly.
Show me the difference between being in love
and loving somebody for real.
I like the idea of belonging with someone
but help me be patient
till I find the right one.
It will have to be somebody
who believes the same for a start
and that's only the beginning.
You'll have to teach us both
more about loving, day by day.
Thanks.
Amen

'You haven't got to go with scrubbers because you might catch things like . . . er . . . nits.'

Thou
shalt not
steal

'I felt gutted when they nicked my bike.'

'I only borrowed it.'

'It was a dare. Now they've dared me to put it back!'

'It fell off the back of a lorry – it was in a shop.'

'I don't know about changing the locks. Maybe they should change the people.'

'If there was no property, would there be no nicking?'

Dear Lord,
Help me to be honest
and for the right reasons;
not just because I'm frightened I'll get caught
nor because the prize isn't big enough.
Help me to be so honest that I wouldn't cheat
if nobody saw and nobody cared.
You'd know – and I would too.
I don't want to think of myself
as a cheat or a thief.
Keep reminding me that however small
it's still stealing.
Help me to remember that if I steal –
someone else loses out somewhere along the line.
It's not the property
it's the people, Lord.
Help me to love others.
Make me sensitive to times when
I'm in danger of spoiling someone's pleasure
or stealing their good name.
It's so easy to take from others
and not even know.

'We all know you shouldn't nick from your mates.
I suppose if we saw all the world as our friends,
we wouldn't nick from anybody.'

GENUINE
DAIRY ICE
CORNISH

9
Thou shalt not
bear false
witness

'Mine's faster than yours. You should have seen me.'

It slipped out of my hand
I don't know anything about it
My dad's bigger than your dad
It was only a white lie
I was only pretending
I didn't mean it
Sorry I was late but the clock didn't go off
I left my homework on the kitchen table
It was only . . .
It was just that . . .
Yes, but . . .
I'm not making excuses but . . .
It was nothing to do with me

Dear Lord,
Forgive me for the lies I have told;
not just the whoppers
but the fibs, the excuses, the white lies,
the gossip, the exaggeration, the boasting,
the tall stories, the pretence
and the lies I've told to myself.
Sometimes I've told the truth
but missed out the awkward bits;
if I meant to mislead
I suppose that was lying too.
I'm sorry.
Forgive me for keeping quiet
when I should have spoken out.
And for not keeping quiet
when I've used the truth to hurt.
I want to be true to you
so help me not to be false to anybody.
In the name of Jesus
who is the Way, the Truth and the Life.
Amen

'It wasn't me, honest.'

10
Thou
shalt not
covet

'Some things I want, I'll never be able to afford; even if I worked all my life. I wouldn't steal them – but I can't help wishing.'

'I don't want any of our next-door-neighbour's things; they're old age pensioners. Anyway, they haven't got any donkeys.'

'I hope my jackpot comes up.'

'Sometimes I've wanted things I didn't really want at all – if I'd thought about it.'

'I reckon all guys want a car, fashion clothes and a girl. I don't know what girls want.'

'There's a lot of greediness in the world.'

'What would I do if I won the pools?'

'I suppose cowboys used to covet guns. Me, I'd settle for a space invader.'

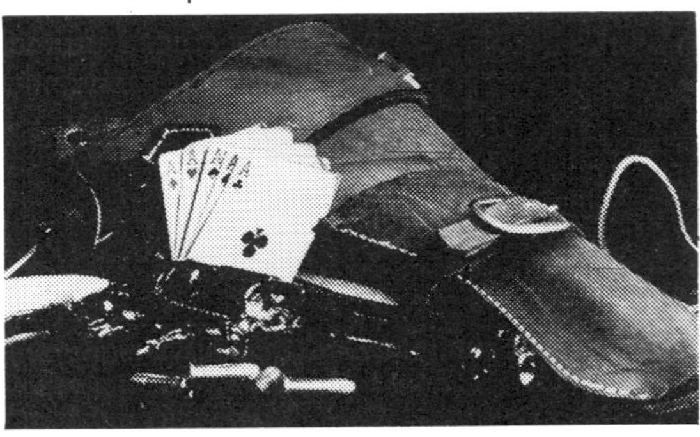

'I wish I was . . .'

'Things.
You thinks you
own them.
But they owns
you.'

'Materialistic society?
Oh you mean the money-god again.
We're back where we started.'

10

Dear Lord,
Forgive me for all the time I've wasted
wishing
for things I haven't got
or to be somebody else
instead of being grateful
for what I have
and glad to be me.
Fretting didn't get me anywhere
it only led me into trouble
and made me dissatisfied.
It took my attention away
from thoughts that really matter.
Help me to recognize jealousy in myself
and to overcome it.

'My nan says she enjoys a little flutter.
She reckons it does her good. With me dad it's
the pigeons. Yeah, there's money in it.
But what's wrong with gambling anyway?'

**Thou shalt love
the Lord thy God
with all thy heart,
and with all thy soul,
and with all thy mind.**

MATTHEW 23:37

'There's more to loving than I bargained for. It's love for your family and for strangers too; it's love for your friends but for your enemies as well; it's love for your lover and for people you don't fancy one little bit. It's love for God too.'

'There's a lot of Nots in these 'ere commandments. The trouble with Nots is it makes you want to do them.'

'The rules Jesus made:
they're harder to keep,
but they're easier to understand.
They're not rules really are they?'

'If I'm tempted to do something, say, but I doesn't do it – don't I get any credit for not going on and doing it? You mean I gets done for just having thought it? That doesn't seem fair to me.'

'It was a better idea to write it on people's hearts instead of on stone because you carry that around with you all the time.'

THE GREATEST COMMANDMENT

Dear Lord,
That Sermon on the Mount –
wow!
The Ten Commandments are hard enough as it is
but if I've got to watch my thoughts as well
– I don't stand a chance.
You didn't make it easier did you?
I mustn't hate anybody
and I must watch out who I fancy –
you've not left me much room –
and that's only two of them.
Even when I did things right
I probably did them for the wrong reasons.
I was busy worrying what not to do
and now I've got to think what I *should* do as well.
I'm sorry but I've failed all round.
You're right though –
the trouble with rules is that you can get round them.
I know I have.
Help me to see behind the letter of each law
to the spirit of its meaning.
Teach me to think behind my actions to the thoughts.
And when I'm stuck wondering what to do –
show me how best to love God
and love my neighbour.

'You knows when
you done wrong.
I don't know how
you knows to know,
but you knows.'

'My New Year resolutions – I can't even remember what they were. Perhaps I'd better start my New Year again today.'

'If you don't listen to your conscience, you don't hear it next time.'

'You punish yourself sometimes. You get regrets. They hurt. If you does a crime you gets punished by the law. If you does a sin you gets punished by yourself.'

'If you're not sorry you gets punished another way. You grows all horrible inside.'

'It's human nature, doing wrong. That doesn't make it right though.'

CONSCIENCE

Dear God,
I still don't know what my conscience is.
Everybody seems to have one.
Is it a bit of you in me?
Help me to listen to it more.
I'm ashamed about
breaking your commandments.
Please forgive me.
I know they're not intended
just to make me feel guilty.
They're meant to help.
Show me how to enjoy trying to keep them.
It should be fun.
Give me a new start
and the power to be different
in Jesus' name.
Amen

'You don't have to have a long face. It can be OK being good.'

WHA
NOW?
'I don't get it
about freedom.
Isn't it just
wanting your own way?
It can't let you off
the rules, can it?'

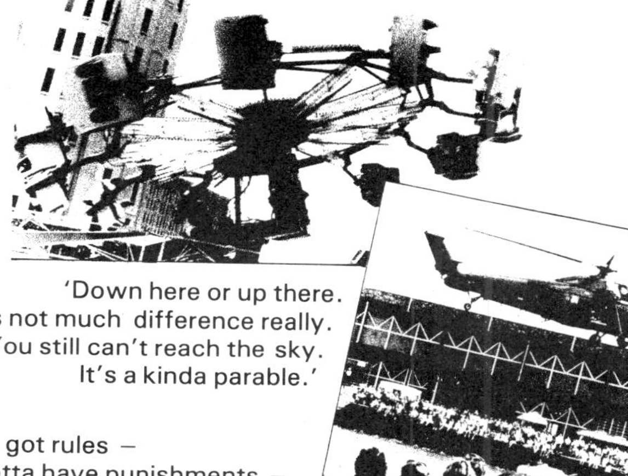

'Down here or up there.
There's not much difference really.
You still can't reach the sky.
It's a kinda parable.'

'If you got rules –
you gotta have punishments –
haven't you?'

'Heaven – that's where God is.
That's all I know about it.'

'There's something fishy about people believing just because they don't want to go to hell. That's based on fear. It's starting off on the wrong foot. I thought it was all supposed to be about love.'

'About these Ten
Commandments.
What do I get
if I win?'

WHAT NOW?

Dear God,
Let's face it –
I've broken them all.
I'm sorry
but that's the way it is.
What now?
Why did you set rules you know we can't keep?
Why did you make me the way I am?
And just say I did keep them all
I still can't win –
I can't buy my way into heaven.
But it's not a prize is it?
It's a gift.
I don't have to deserve a gift.
I just have to believe.
Is that all there is to it?
But isn't believing earning it?
I don't understand
but I'll take your word for it.
I like what it teaches in the New Testament,
about Jesus making a New Covenant and giving
us a fresh start.
And I like the idea of eternal life
beginning now.
So whatever the deal is,
count me in.

'At this rate, nobody'll ever get in.'

**Dear Lord,
I've given up
trying to sus out
these Ten Commandments.
I'll try to keep them
just because you
want me to.**

New English Bible
New
English
Bible

THE TEN COMMANDMENTS

taken from the Good News Bible

God spoke, and these were his words:
'I am the Lord your God who brought you out of Egypt, where you were slaves.
1 Worship no god but me.
2 Do not make for yourselves images of anything in heaven or on earth or in the water under the earth. Do not bow down to any idol or worship it, because I am the Lord your God and I tolerate no rivals. I bring punishment on those who hate me and on their descendants down to the third and fourth generation. But I show my love to thousands of generations of those who love me and obey my laws.
3 Do not use my name for evil purposes, because I, the Lord your God, will punish anyone who misuses my name.
4 Observe the Sabbath and keep it holy. You have six days in which to do your work, but the seventh day is a day of rest dedicated to me. On that day no one is to work – neither you, your children, your slaves, your animals, nor the foreigners who live in your country. In six days I, the Lord, made the earth, the sky, the sea, and everything in them, but on the seventh day I rested. That is why I, the Lord, blessed the Sabbath and made it holy.
5 Respect your father and your mother, so that you may live a long time in the land that I am giving you.
6 Do not commit murder.
7 Do not commit adultery.
8 Do not steal.
9 Do not accuse anyone falsely.
10 Do not desire another man's house; do not desire his wife, his slaves, his cattle, his donkeys, or anything else that he owns.'

Exodus 20:1–17

Appendix

Bible references to the 'conflict stories' (see p. 10)
Authority to forgive sins *Mark 2:1–12*
Eating with sinners *Mark 2:13–17*
Fasting *Mark 2:18–22*
Cornfields on the sabbath *Mark 2:23–28*
The man with the withered arm *Mark 3:1–6*
The Beelzebub controversy *Mark 3:20–30, Luke 11:14–36*
Washing hands *Mark 7:1–23, Luke 11:37–54*

Luke has two more sabbath stories:
The crippled woman *Luke 13:10–17*
The man who had dropsy *Luke 14:1–6*

There were more arguments in the last week of Jesus' life:
About authority followed by a story *Mark 11:27 – 12:12*
About paying taxes *Mark 12:13–17*
About religious arguments over the resurrection of the dead *Mark 12:18–27*
About the greatest commandment *Mark 12:28–34*
About the Messiah, followed by Jesus' comment on religious practices *Mark 12:35–44*

John has two conflict stories that took place on the sabbath:
The argument that began with carrying a bed on the sabbath *John 5:1–18*
The argument about true sight that began with a blind man being healed on the sabbath *John 9*

Jesus and the Law:
The Sermon on the Mount *Matthew 5, 6 and 7*
The Transfiguration *Mark 9:2–8*
The New Covenant *Jeremiah 31:31–34*
The Last Supper *1 Corinthians 11:23–25*

'Do not suppose that I have come to abolish the Law and the prophets: I did not come to abolish but to complete.'
Matthew 5:17

Acknowledgements

Cover photograph: Lion Publishing/Jon Willcocks
Text photographs: Andrew Beese with Michael Gazzard, Ian Hayes, Salman Bhaidani, Derek Brimble and Mark Grimes. Thanks to Ron Rogers, Head of Photography Department, Greenway School and Press Gang Printing Co. 60 Redcliffe St., Bristol for use of facilities

Special thanks to: Ian Hayes, Anthony O'Reilly, Richard Jaap, Iain Barron, Neil Marsh, Salman Bhaidani, Glenroy Henry, Robert Welsman, Richard Long, Alistair Johnstone, Martin Hill, Mortimer Boyce, Ian Hannan, Paul Slade, Kevin Humphries, Marcus Humphries, Bobby Stenner, Michael Russell, John Paisey, Jason Holloway, Michael Oakes, Alan Sharp, Chris Saunders, Dean Hartley, Paul Sanki, John Cook, Larry Wollacott, Martin Melnyk, David Atwell, Raymond Beattie, Andrew Lear, Paul Griffiths, Declan Ainger, Keith Davis, Christopher Jarrett, Scott Mitchard, Vicki Shaw, Rosemary Gerrish, Mark Packer, Paul Gilmore and P. Godfrey, Headmaster